D1002199

Pompeii

Essential Library
An Imprint of Abdo Publishing | www.abdopublishing.com

DIGGING UP
the Past

Pompeii

Huntington City
Township Public Library
255 West Park Drive
Huntington, IN 46750

BY DIANE MARCZELY GIMPEL

CONTENT CONSULTANT
J. CLAYTON FANT
PROFESSOR OF CLASSICAL STUDIES
UNIVERSITY OF AKRON

www.abdopublishing.com

Published by Abdo Publishing, a division of ABDO, PO Box 398166, Minneapolis, Minnesota 55439. Copyright © 2015 by Abdo Consulting Group, Inc. International copyrights reserved in all countries. No part of this book may be reproduced in any form without written permission from the publisher. Essential Library™ is a trademark and logo of Abdo Publishing.

Printed in the United States of America, North Mankato, Minnesota
032014
092014

THIS BOOK CONTAINS
RECYCLED MATERIALS

Cover Photo: Arthur R./Shutterstock Images
Interior Photos: Arthur R./Shutterstock Images, 2; Karl Briullov, 6; Fesenko Ievgenii/Shutterstock Images, 10; iStock/Thinkstock, 13; Atlaspix/Shutterstock Images, 13 (inset); Joseph Wright of Derby, 15; Bettmann/Corbis, 16, 44; H. M. Herget/National Geographic Image Collection/Glow Images, 19; Henry J. Pain/Corbis, 21; ImageBroker/Glow Images, 25; CM Dixon/Heritage Images/Glow Images, 27, 67; Shutterstock Images, 30, 32, 61; Raimund Kutter/ImageBroker/Glow Images, 35; Historical/Glow Images, 37; Corbis, 42; Werner Forman Archive/Glow Images, 48, 79; SuperStock/Glow Images, 50, 58; Drimi/Shutterstock Images, 53; BAO/ImageBroker/Glow Images, 54, 64, 80; Nadar, 60; Sean Sexton Collection/Corbis, 63, 76; Werner Forman Archive/Heritage Images/Glow Images, 69; De Agostini/Getty Images, 71; US Army Air Forces, 83; Jonathan Blair/Corbis, 87; Salvatore Laporta/AP Images, 88; Luigi Nifosì/Tips RM/Glow Images, 92; Andrea Muscatello/Shutterstock Images, 97

Editor: Arnold Ringstad
Series Designer: Becky Daum

Library of Congress Control Number: 2014932250

Cataloging-in-Publication Data

Gimpel, Diane Marczely.
 Pompeii / Diane Marczely Gimpel.
  p. cm. -- (Digging up the past)
Includes bibliographical references and index.
ISBN 978-1-62403-236-3
1. Pompeii (Extinct city)--Juvenile literature. 2. Vesuvius (Italy)--Eruption, 79--Juvenile literature. 3. Excavations (Archaeology)--Italy--Pompeii (Extinct city)--Juvenile literature. I. Title.
937--dc23

                                          2014932250

CONTENTS

Why Pompeii Matters Today

In 79 CE, Mount Vesuvius in southern Italy exploded.
The eruption of the volcano spelled destruction
for many people who lived at the base of Vesuvius,
including thousands in a city called Pompeii. Pompeii
seemed to be wiped from the face of the Earth,
buried under the tons of ash and rock spewed
during the eruption. Pompeii's existence as a vibrant
city full of residents, tourists, and businesspeople
ended abruptly.

The eruption of Vesuvius has captured the imagination of artists for centuries.

However, although its people fled or died, Pompeii did not perish permanently as a result of Vesuvius' wrath. The work of archaeologists and excavators has brought Pompeii back to life over the course of hundreds of years, many centuries after the city's last residents died.

SIGNALS OF DOOM

Scientists now know the eruption of Mount Vesuvius should not have been the surprise it was to the residents of Pompeii. There were warnings from the volcano before it exploded. Earthquakes shook Campania, the area in southern Italy where Vesuvius is located, for several days before the eruption. Still, the residents, visitors, and workers in the region did not leave. Earthquakes were common in the area. Now, scientists know there may be a connection between earthquakes and volcanic eruptions. They pay special attention to the vibrations of the earth around volcanoes.

ANCIENT LIFE PRESERVED

Pompeii's destruction was a tragedy for its citizens. But the city's volcanic demise gives archaeologists an unprecedented glimpse into the way people lived in ancient times. "If an ancient city survives to become a modern city, like Naples, its readability in archaeological terms is enormously reduced," says scholar Andrew Wallace-Hadrill. "It's a paradox of archaeology: you read the past best in its moments of trauma."[1] In other words, cities typically evolve over time, shedding much of their past in the process. Ancient cities were toppled by nature or war, ransacked by looters, or simply built over as residents used old buildings for new purposes and constructed new structures. But Pompeii's sudden end offers a relatively pure view of the past. The huge amounts of rock and ash that came from Mount Vesuvius completely buried the town. However, Pompeii was not, as popular accounts sometimes claim, simply frozen in time. Its natural preservation was uneven, and looting and recovery efforts throughout the centuries have significantly altered parts of the ruins.

Still, Pompeii's burial makes it an excellent place to learn about the ancient world. CyArk, an organization that aims to digitally preserve cultural heritage sites like Pompeii, makes this point:

> *Pompeii is an indispensable resource for understanding the complex fabric of the classical world. The architecture and urbanism of Pompeii reveals pre-Roman, colonial Roman, and imperial Roman building traditions. . . . Only in Pompeii is it possible to trace the history of Italian and Roman domestic architecture for at least four centuries.*[2]

Knowledge of Italian and Roman history is important to understand how the world operates today. Many of the Western world's institutions, cultures, and philosophies are rooted in the classical Roman world.

POMPEII AND SOCIETY

Glimpses into the ancient world of Pompeii fueled modern imaginations. When archaeologists first exposed parts of the city in the large, state-sponsored excavations of the 1700s, Pompeii caught the attention of Enlightenment thinkers. Followers of the movement believed in using the scientific method for learning rather than relying on faith or superstition. The information gleaned from Pompeii inspired them to reflect on the ancient city and incorporate aspects of it into their modern lives. As archaeologist Salvatore Ciro Nappo notes, "Slowly a new, Neo-classical, attitude emerged, influencing philosophers, men of letters, and artists. Painters, sculptors, jewelers, upholsterers, cabinet-makers, joiners, decorators—all made explicit reference to the findings in the towns that Vesuvius buried."[3]

Pompeii even had an impact on home decorating in the 1700s. Ancient Roman styles found their way into many homes of the day.

The amazing preservation of Pompeii's buildings, including the Temple of Isis, makes the city one of the most important archaeological sites on Earth.

Between the 1600s and the 1800s, it was a custom for young, wealthy men with a classical education in Greek and Latin to travel through the old cities of Europe. They often began in London and made mandatory stops in Paris and Rome. Along with France and Italy, men making the Grand Tour also might stop in the Netherlands, Switzerland, Germany, Spain, Greece, and Turkey. The young men would travel with a teacher or a guardian and were expected to return home with a better understanding of art and architecture, as well as souvenirs from their travels.

The wealthy displayed reproductions of objects and art found at Pompeii. Some even styled their entire houses after the ancient Italian finds. European elites sent their sons to Pompeii as part of the cultural and educational journey through Europe known as the Grand Tour. Viewing evidence of the past and understanding it was seen as essential to becoming a person of influence.

POMPEII AND ARCHAEOLOGY

The excavations at Pompeii and the other cities buried by Vesuvius marked the beginning of the modern science of archaeology. Pompeii was one of the first major ancient sites where archaeologists used systematic and professional methods to conduct their work. Many modern principles of archaeology were established as a result of the work done at Pompeii. Today, scientists studying Pompeii are on the cutting edge of the best archaeological and preservation practices.

Early in the history of archaeology, people preserved ancient objects by simply removing them from a site and installing them in a museum. Later, scientists believed in preserving the original sites as closely as possible to the way they were found. Modern archaeologists prefer preservation over the treasure-hunting methods of the past.

WHERE IS POMPEII?

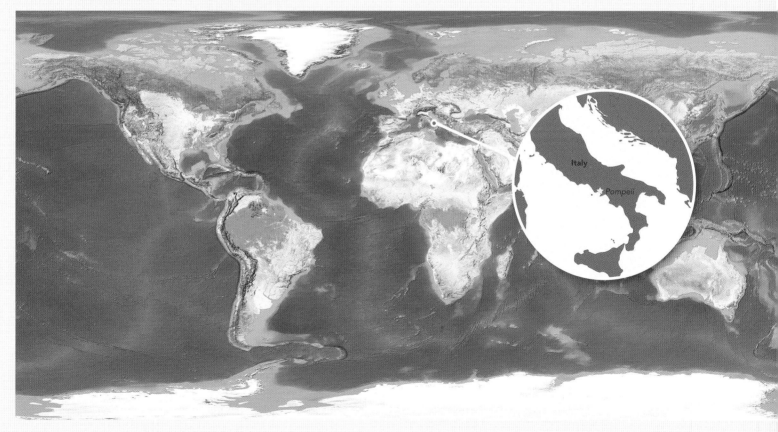

POMPEII AND VOLCANOLOGY

More people than just archaeologists benefit from the lessons of Pompeii. Scientists who study volcanoes also learn a great deal from the site. The well-preserved city gives researchers a unique laboratory where they can study the effects of eruptions on buildings and people. Studying past eruptions gives scientists a better idea of how to survive future volcanoes. It also provides clues about how to predict when eruptions will happen. Eyewitnesses to the 79 eruption recorded detailed information about the behavior of Mount Vesuvius in the days, months, and years leading up to the disaster.

Some terms used in the science of volcanology are rooted

OLYMPIA: ANOTHER BURIED TREASURE

Pompeii is not the only abandoned, buried, and excavated place on Earth. Olympia, Greece, home of the original Olympic Games, is another. Olympia was primarily a pagan religious center. Its first sanctuary to Greek deities was established in approximately 1000 BCE. Earthquakes and mudslides buried the city, leading to Olympia's abandonment. An English archaeologist discovered the ruins in 1776, and the French partially excavated a temple to the Greek god Zeus in 1829. Large-scale excavations began in 1875 under German direction.[4]

in studies of the Pompeii disaster. Plinian eruptions are named after Pliny the Younger, a man who witnessed and described the eruption of Mount Vesuvius in 79. The eruptions are distinguished by very tall columns of ash and the ejection of large amounts of volcanic rock.

Scholars have used eyewitness accounts and scientific data to reconstruct Vesuvius's apocalyptic eruption.

The Burial of Pompeii

Pompeii became a Roman colony in 80 BCE. By the dawn of the first millennium CE, it was a coastal city of approximately 12,000 residents. Located in western Italy not far from the city of Naples, Pompeii lay adjacent to the Mediterranean Sea and the Sarno River. The dominant feature of the city's surroundings was Vesuvius, a 4,203-foot (1,281 m) mountain located to the northwest.[1]

Pompeii's ornately decorated buildings and bustling populace had survived previous natural disasters, but the 79 eruption would signal the city's demise.

LIFE IN POMPEII

Pompeii thrived economically during its heyday, and a number of industries flourished there. Among those industries was agriculture, which benefited from the area's fertile volcanic soil and mild climate. Farmers grew olives for oil, and the town was famous for its wine and *garum*, a type of fermented fish sauce. Sheepherders did strong business in meat, milk, and wool. Wool was cleaned, dyed, and woven into cloth in Pompeian felt factories. Traders did well in Pompeii because the city's location near the Mediterranean Sea gave them access to many markets. People have found wine from ancient Pompeii as far away as France, Spain, and North Africa, demonstrating the city's trading power. Ancient Pompeii was also a tourism hub. Wealthy Romans vacationed in Pompeii, taking in the sun, sea, and scenery. The retail industry thrived, too. Tourists and the full-time residents of Pompeii patronized local businesses, including various shops and taverns. Historians believe most bathhouses were public and free, though people often conducted business within them. Many of these establishments were found on the main shopping street, now called the Via dell'Abbondanza.

Residents of Pompeii woke with the sun, ate a breakfast of bread and cheese, and headed off to work. Citizens owned manufacturing firms, tilled farms, or waited on customers in shops. Slaves performed daily labor. Work began very early in the day. As a result, the early afternoon was time for a

By 79 CE, the Roman Empire had entered a centuries-long period of peace and prosperity.

meal and a rest. On public festival days, many people went to the amphitheater for a gladiator contest.

Bath time also took place in the afternoon. Residents and slaves relaxed at communal baths, which offered hot and cold water, as well as a place to socialize, exercise, and do business. Just before sunset, the Romans had a dinner of olives, eggs, and fish or meat, prepared in a small kitchen at the back of the house. Only large homes had dedicated kitchens. In smaller houses, people simply used portable cookware over a fire.

Vesuvius has produced many eruptions; the one that buried Pompeii in 79 CE was not the first. Scientists believe the caldera of Mount Vesuvius formed following an eruption 17,000 years ago.[7] In approximately 6940 BCE and 2420 BCE, Vesuvius experienced large eruptions. During an eruption in 1780 BCE, thousands of people ran in panic from destruction that reached as far as 15 miles (24 km) away.[8] Archaeologists found ash tracks of thousands of footprints leading away from the volcano.

ERUPTION

On August 20, 79 CE, the ground began shaking in Pompeii. The quakes continued for four days. Then, on August 24, at approximately 1:00 p.m., Mount Vesuvius erupted.[2] The pressure of the eruption blew off a plug of rock that had sealed the volcano, spewing pumice and ash more than nine miles (15 km) into the air.[3] Pliny the Younger, a young man who was staying with his mother and his uncle, Pliny the Elder, in nearby Misenum, recorded an eyewitness account. He wrote that the brown plume shooting up from the volcano looked like a pine tree, "for carried up to a very great height as if on a tree-trunk, it began to spread out into various branches."[4] The cloud, Pliny wrote, was "[sometimes] white, sometimes dirty and speckled, according to how much soil and ash it carried."[5] The wind carried the plume to nearby Pompeii, which was pelted with rocks and darkened by the ash cloud approximately a half hour after the explosion. Debris rained upon Pompeii for 18 hours as the plume grew to more than 18 miles (30 km) high.[6] During the harshest part of the eruption, Vesuvius ejected more than 165,000 short tons (150,000 metric tons) of material per second. The drifting debris piled up in Pompeii to a depth of almost 10 feet (3 m).[9] The ash and rock buried buildings and filled their interiors. Some people died when roofs collapsed under the weight. Others were killed when they were hit by falling debris as they tried to run away. Some of the people who fled covered their heads with pillows for protection. The ground continued to rumble, and fires blazed on the mountain. Despite the ruined appearance of the town, most people in Pompeii survived the initial blast.

AUGUST 25

The survivors did not last long. The next morning, on August 25, Vesuvius let loose a pyroclastic

Pliny's vivid descriptions made it possible for later artists to portray the eruption's destructive effects.

PLINY THE ELDER

Pliny the Elder was a Roman scholar and naturalist. He became known to historians primarily for two things: his authorship of the encyclopedia *Historia Naturalis* and his death in the eruption of Mount Vesuvius. When Vesuvius erupted, Pliny the Elder, who also was the commander of the Roman fleet at Misenum, took a ship to the other side of the Bay of Naples. His goal was to rescue his friends and get a closer look at the explosion. He died the next day on the shores of the bay at Stabiae, possibly from suffocating on toxic fumes.

flow that traveled down the mountain at more than 60 miles per hour (97 kmh).[10] The surge did not reach Pompeii, but subsequent surges reached farther beyond the mountain. Finally, the fourth surge of 750-degree-Fahrenheit (400°C) gas, rock, and ash reached Pompeii.[11] It struck the fatal blow to thousands of people in the city and the surrounding areas. The surge instantly killed those it hit, boiling them in a searing blast of heat. Those who were farther from the hottest part of the flow suffocated when they breathed in hot ash and toxic gases.

From Misenum, today an hour's drive from Pompeii on the other side of the Bay of Naples, Pliny the Younger described the surge as a black cloud broken with zigzag flashes that looked like lightning with masses of flame behind it. The ground shook violently, causing tsunamis with rushing waves that left some sea animals uncovered by water. Pliny recounted that people began to panic and run away as a cloud descended on Misenum, darkening the city. He wrote:

You could hear women screaming, babies wailing, men shouting: some were calling out for their parents, others for their children, others for their spouses, and trying to recognize their voices; some lamented their own misfortune, others that of their relatives; there were some who in their fear of dying prayed for death; many raised their hands to the gods; more still concluded that there were no gods and that this was the world's final and everlasting night.[12]

The Misenum residents survived, however, and returned to their town. Everything was so densely covered in ash that it looked like there had been a heavy snowfall.

By the time the eruption ended late in the afternoon of August 25, a layer of ash and pumice 19 to 23 feet (6 to 7 m) deep covered Pompeii.[13] The entire city was buried, making the area look like it had never before seen civilization. Sunlight, which had been blotted out by the volcanic cloud, returned to the area on the third day. People traveled to the once-bustling city to see what they could find.

PLINY'S LETTERS

Gaius Plinius Caecilius Secundus, better known as Pliny the Younger, was 18 years old when he watched from Misenum as Mount Vesuvius erupted in 79 CE. Pliny was living with Pliny the Elder, his uncle and adoptive father, following the death of Pliny's natural father some years before. Years after the eruption, Pliny the Younger described the blast in two letters to historian Cornelius Tacitus. During his career as a lawyer and author, Pliny wrote hundreds of letters on various subjects to many people, including Roman emperors. A scholar discovered the letters in the 1500s. They offer a unique glimpse into ancient Roman life.

3

Digging Begins

After the eruption, Mount Vesuvius continued to spew ash and rock for several days. Ash the volcano sent into the atmosphere partially blocked the sun for months. Still, people returned to the city to assess the damage. They found a barren plain covered with dark ash, punctuated in places by a rooftop poking through the surface. Below the surface stood the remains of the city—and of those who perished within it.

The first excavators of Pompeii were the returning residents of the city and nearby areas.

THE FIRST DIGGERS

Among the first to arrive after the eruption were evacuees looking for their houses and possessions. The survivors were the first to dig at Pompeii and may have searched for material they could reuse, such as bronze, lead, and marble. They likely were joined by looters looking for the same things. Archaeologists debate the extent of these early searches, but there is evidence that at least a few people returned to investigate the ruins. One message found scrawled on a wall read, "house tunneled through," indicating someone had explored the ruins after the disaster.[1]

The shafts the earliest excavators used to enter and leave the city were flimsy, dark, and narrow. Diggers used hand-pumped bellows to send fresh air underground. Many—including children sent in as scouts—wound up buried alongside the victims of the original eruption. Later, archaeologists discovered Roman coins dating from the 300s in the depths of the ruins, confirming tunnel diggers were buried alive long after the catastrophe in 79 CE.

THE GOVERNMENT ARRIVES

The Roman emperor Titus sent two government workers to Pompeii soon after the devastation. They were tasked with assessing the damage and organizing aid for the surviving residents of the region. Titus, who became

In addition to the disaster at Pompeii, Titus also dealt with a large fire in Rome in the spring of 80.

emperor just two months before the disaster, declared a state of emergency and offered funding for cleanup and recovery efforts. His actions were similar to those taken by governments today following severe natural disasters. However, some of the funding for Pompeii's recovery was obtained by taking the property of people known to have died in the disaster.

The salvagers went through the accessible ruins and removed objects they valued. Exactly what they took remains unclear.

Today, it is difficult or even impossible to completely distinguish ancient salvaging operations from ones carried out more than 1,000 years later. Consequently, although Pompeii eventually became one of the richest archaeological finds in history, it was ransacked long before modern archaeologists uncovered it. Titus visited the disaster area himself in 80. He wanted to rebuild the cities affected by the Vesuvius eruption. However, after viewing the aftermath, the emperor decided not to uncover Pompeii and the other buried towns in the region. Titus may have abandoned the idea because he determined the value to be gained by uncovering and rebuilding the towns would not offset the cost of such a massive project. In addition, the empire had neither the knowledge nor the technology to do a restoration. The feat would be incredibly difficult even today. The decision of the emperor and the residents to abandon Pompeii emphasizes how catastrophic the eruption was to the region. The Romans typically would rebuild after disasters such as massive earthquakes.

EMPEROR TITUS

Titus became the ruler of the Roman Empire in June of 79 following the death of his father, Emperor Vespasian. Titus is known primarily for destroying and conquering the city of Jerusalem in 70 while working as a military commander for his father. The Arch of Titus, built in 81 to memorialize the victory, still stands at the entrance to the Roman Forum. Titus is also known for helping the Pompeii region financially after the Vesuvian eruption and for completing the Roman Colosseum. Titus ruled until his death in 81.

LATER ERUPTIONS

For centuries, Pompeii lay silent under tons of ash. Mount Vesuvius, however, was not quiet. It continued to erupt over the ensuing decades and centuries.

The Roman physician and philosopher Galen wrote of the volcano burning in 172. Roman historian Dio Cassius reported another Vesuvian explosion in 203. Historian Marcellinus Comes wrote about an eruption on November 6, 472, that "caused night during the day and covered all Europe with fine ash."[2]

POMPEII'S EARLIER DISASTER

The devastation caused by Mount Vesuvius in 79 was not Pompeii's first experience with a catastrophe. In approximately 62, an earthquake shook the city. In some places, houses were completely leveled. In other spots, the top floors of buildings were badly damaged.

Following the earthquake, the residents of Pompeii worked to rebuild. They had to reestablish the city's water supply and rebuild the Temple of Isis. Archaeologists once believed Pompeii was in a state of neglect when Mount Vesuvius erupted in 79. Now, most archaeologists believe the residents simply had not finished the restoration of the city by the time the volcano erupted.

Additional eruptions occurred in 685, 787, 968, 1037, sometime between 1068 and 1078, and again in 1139 and 1500. However, none of these eruptions came close to the size of the one that buried Pompeii. Vesuvius's eruptions are variable in scope. Some have consisted of simple oozing lava, while others have resulted in enormous explosions of ash and rock. Vesuvius's next big blast happened in 1631, after the discovery of Pompeii.

WHAT CAME OUT OF VESUVIUS?

Several substances came out of Mount Vesuvius when it erupted in 79 CE. Among them was basalt, a type of volcanic rock. Earlier volcanic eruptions had provided the rock ancient Romans used to pave roads in Pompeii and Rome. Pumice, a light volcanic rock filled with pores from gas bubbles, also spewed from Vesuvius.

The Romans occasionally used it as a construction material. Today, pumice is useful in household cleaning supplies and personal grooming products because of its abrasiveness. Vesuvius also expelled hot gases, as well as other types of volcanic rock and ash, known as lapilli and tephra.

Vesuvius's crater appears peaceful when the volcano is dormant, but its activity once every few centuries gives the volcano its fearsome reputation.

4

Buried Cities

Builders accidentally discovered Pompeii in the late 1500s during the construction of a water diversion project. Count Muzzio Tuttavilla wanted to send water from the nearby Sarno River to his villa in Torre Annunziata. He also wanted to divert water to a weapons factory in the same area. Architect Domenico Fontana designed an underground channel for the project. When planning the project, he did not realize the channel would go directly through Pompeii.

Statues and other works of art were among the first discoveries at the Pompeii ruins.

THE FIRST FIND

As workers dug the channel between 1592 and 1600, they found walls covered in marble and frescoes. Workers also found statues with inscriptions written in Latin, the language of Roman citizens in the first century CE. One of the inscriptions bore the word *pompeis*, which was incorrectly interpreted to refer to the villa of a Roman general named Pompey rather than to the city of Pompeii. Fontana, however, was convinced he had entered the ancient city of Pompeii.

Fontana asked to explore the city further, but his employer said no. He ordered Fontana to bury the objects he had uncovered. Fontana, who had found other buried Roman villas during the course of his job, recorded his find and moved on. The modern field of archaeology had not developed yet, so there was no framework for a thorough investigation of the site. Fontana simply continued with the water diversion project.

In 1631, Mount Vesuvius erupted violently again. After months of earthquakes, a Plinian eruption destroyed nearby villages and killed thousands of people. A few years later, German scholar Lucas Holstenius determined Pompeii had once stood in the place near Vesuvius known as La Civita. However, his peers refused to believe him.

DOMENICO FONTANA

Domenico Fontana, who found Pompeii in the late 1500s as he built a water channel through the buried city, was an Italian architect who once held the job of architect for the pope of the Roman Catholic Church. Fontana designed the Vatican Library and worked on the completion of the dome of Saint Peter's Basilica, which was designed by Michelangelo. After Pope Clement VIII fired him in 1592 for allegedly mishandling funds, Fontana signed on to the water diversion project in Naples.

In one of his most famous projects, he moved an Egyptian column originally brought to Rome in the first century CE to a position in front of Saint Peter's Basilica. Fontana died in 1607 in Naples, Italy.

The ornate Vatican Library is among Fontana's best-known works.

Huntington City
Township Public Library
255 West Park Drive
Huntington, IN 46750

ANOTHER FIND

In 1689, workers digging a well discovered buried walls covered in inscriptions. One inscription included the word *Pompei*. As with Fontana's workers, most believed the writing referred to General Pompey rather than Pompeii, so it was largely ignored.

A few years later, scholar Giuseppe Macrini, who was studying Mount Vesuvius, did some exploratory digging of his own at the site and saw the frescoes himself. He published his findings in 1699, claiming Pompeii was buried beneath the area known as La Civita. But most scholars did not believe him or anyone else who claimed Pompeii was underground.

A SISTER CITY IS DISCOVERED

In the early 1700s, a prince refuted the idea that there were no cities buried by Vesuvius. In 1709, a worker digging a well found chunks of marble in Herculaneum, a city north of Pompeii. Word of the find reached Austrian prince Emmanuel Maurice d'Elbeuf, who was married to a princess from the Kingdom of Naples. Construction was currently underway on his new seaside home in the area. He bought the land in Herculaneum so he could use the marble to decorate his new home.

The prince suspected the marble was not simply dug from the earth but had been used on ancient buildings. He was correct. The marble had come from Herculaneum's theater. He launched the first organized excavation of a town buried by Vesuvius during the 79 eruption. His aim was simply to decorate his new house with ancient treasures. The prince saw no need to document his findings. He simply ignored or destroyed unwanted items.

The dig focused on Herculaneum's theater, which the prince thought was Hercules's temple. Among the first artifacts removed was a statue of Hercules, along with a statue of three women. The prince gave the statues to Prince Eugene, his cousin in Vienna, Austria. He kept most of the other treasures for himself. Workers toiled in narrow, dark, and dank tunnels lit

Excavations at Herculaneum attracted archaeological interest to the region.

only by smoky torches. They breathed the small amounts of fresh air coming in from below the well. The diggers created horizontal channels moving out from the original well and mined the theater for marble and statues. In 1716, workers sealed the tunnel, and excavation stopped once the prince's villa was complete. The Roman Catholic Church, headquartered in Rome and holding significant political power in the region, disapproved of smuggling ancient art out of Italy.

A BRIEF HISTORY OF HERCULANEUM

Herculaneum gets its name from the Greek hero Heracles, later renamed Hercules by the Romans. It was founded in the 500s BCE by Samnite tribes native to Italy. Soon after its founding, however, Herculaneum came under Greek control, where it remained until the Samnites wrested it away again in the 300s BCE. Herculaneum became a Roman municipality in 89 BCE.

Mount Vesuvius buried Herculaneum in up to 60 feet (18 m) of ash and volcanic mud in 79.[1] The mud hardened, which made Herculaneum more difficult to uncover than Pompeii. However, the hardness and depth of the volcanic material kept Herculaneum out of the hands of looters and preserved the upper stories of buildings, unlike those in Pompeii.

A LARGE-SCALE EXCAVATION

Political change in the first half of the 1700s led to the first full-scale excavation of the buried cities of Campania. After Prince Eugene of Austria died, the statues given to him by his cousin were sold to the king of Poland. The king's daughter, Maria Amalia, married Charles of Bourbon, who later became King Charles VII of Naples. Maria Amalia, who had seen the statues from Herculaneum acquired by her father, may have urged her husband to dig for more now that they were living in the area. Additionally, for European royalty, gathering and exhibiting ancient art was a display of power. Charles would have been interested in showing off ancient treasures to enhance the prestige of his newly established rule. Charles intended for the finds to be treated as part of a royal collection that would remain with the kingdom rather than being sold off to a private collector for possible removal from the country.

Charles hired Roque Joachim de Alcubierre, a Spanish military engineer, to do the excavation.

THE HERCULANEUM THEATER

The Herculaneum Theater is a semicircular structure with a diameter of more than 111 feet (34 m) and capacity to hold 2,500 people—approximately half the population of the town.[2] Spectators sat upon stone seats that descended to the orchestra pit. They reached the seats by using one of seven sets of stairways. The stairways cut the tiers of seats into six wedges, like pieces of pie. The theater was decorated with marble, columns, and bronze statues, but most of its decorations were stripped away during the excavations of the 1700s.

Alcubierre was not an archaeologist, so recording his findings and conserving the underground city were not important to him. His job was simply to recover marble statues, mosaics, wall panels, and other portable treasures.

To get to the treasures, Alcubierre went in through existing wells, then tunneled through the city's ancient walls, smashing frescoes. The tunnels were barely large enough for a worker to pass through and sometimes collapsed. Water and slime came out of the walls when workers chipped away at their hardened volcanic deposits. Workers were trapped in darkness when their oil lamps or smoky torches went out. Forced to dig, the workers were chained

CHARLES OF BOURBON

Charles of Bourbon became the king of Naples in 1734 and commissioned the first state excavations of Herculaneum and Pompeii soon after ascending to the throne. Twenty-five years later, he turned Naples over to his son and became king of Spain following the death of his half brother, the previous king of Spain.

As king of Spain, Charles did not have a successful foreign policy. He found himself in a war against England. As a result, Spain lost Florida to the British. However, Charles managed to improve Spain's trade. When he died in 1788, Spain was in a better economic state than when Charles first became king.

so they could not escape the horrible conditions and to prevent them from thieving.

PAVING THE WAY TO POMPEII

Alcubierre was criticized for the destruction he caused to Herculaneum, but change did not come until he became ill and a French engineer named Pierre Bardet de Villeneuve was appointed director of excavations. He tunneled along street lines rather than through walls. He also cleared the area around some buildings, including the basilica, homes, and commercial structures.

Alcubierre eventually returned from sick leave and continued excavating the way he always had: tunneling through walls and filling old tunnels with the debris from digging new tunnels. However, he began keeping an inventory of his finds. Eventually, the treasures at Herculaneum were depleted, and Alcubierre turned his sights on nearby Pompeii.

5

Pompeii's First Big Dig

As the number of treasures pulled out of Herculaneum decreased, Alcubierre moved his team to another hill in the vicinity of Mount Vesuvius. The new location was known as La Civita, and a few frescoes and other ancient objects were reportedly uncovered there. Fontana had supposedly found ancient treasures in the underground canal he dug more than 100 years earlier. Alcubierre wanted to keep sending treasure to the man who hired him, King Charles of Naples, so he could keep his job.

Removing ash and debris required enormous amounts of labor in the days before modern excavation technology.

He decided to see what he could find under the hill.

DIGGING AT POMPEII BEGINS

Alcubierre took 24 men, half of whom were criminals, to the site and began digging on March 23, 1748.[1] It was relatively easy to dig because the material piled on top of Pompeii was different from the material at Herculaneum. First, there was less of it. Pompeii was buried by approximately 13 feet (4 m) of volcanic debris, while parts of Herculaneum were

The digs at Pompeii began slowly, accelerating only once techniques were refined and the workforce grew.

buried by 75 feet (23 m), some of which was deposited by the 1631 eruption of Vesuvius.[2] In addition, most of the debris covering Pompeii was soft ash and loose volcanic rocks, while the volcanic mud covering Herculaneum had hardened like concrete, making it difficult to dig.

Still, the excavation of Pompeii presented problems to the workers. One hazard was loose volcanic matter. Workers could fall into it and become trapped. Another hazard was *mofeta*, pockets of poisonous gas trapped in the layers of volcanic ash. Once released, the mofeta could kill if inhaled. Fear of mofeta sometimes caused workers to stop digging.

FIRST FINDS

Despite the dangers and work stoppages, the excavation continued. The first large structure Alcubierre's team discovered was the amphitheater, which bears some similarity to modern sports stadiums. Also discovered was the necropolis, a graveyard by the Herculaneum Gate. Workers found the first human skeleton on April 19, 1748.

Alcubierre's job, as he saw it, was to find art and send it to Naples for the king's national museum, not to preserve or study the site. Because of this perspective, his team permanently damaged Pompeii in some places and destroyed it in others during their excavations in the 1700s. They stripped away frescoes, statues, columns, and even streets. The team removed all objects of value at a dig site. Then, they filled in the site with debris from the next dig site.

Camillo Paderni, curator of the king's museum in Portici, decided which items were beautiful enough to be part of the royal collection. If the excavators found wall paintings deemed unworthy of placement in the national museum, they knocked them down. The excavators used hammers to destroy objects they considered common because there was no place to keep them.

NEW EXCAVATOR, NEW METHODS

In 1750, Swiss engineer Karl Weber joined King Charles's excavation team and began documenting the buildings and objects found in Pompeii. Regarding this new approach, modern researcher Lale Özgenel wrote:

> *Weber's era is particularly noteworthy in this first phase of excavations in terms of preparing the first collection of documents on Vesuvian archaeology. . . . For the first time since the official inception of the excavations. . . Weber approached the work and the site with an archaeological perspective.[3]*

Özgenel contended Weber's predecessor at Pompeii, Alcubierre, "was far from shedding light on the context of the ancient city; in no way did he aim to unearth the sites in a systematic way to expose the well-preserved urban fabric."[4] Weber had a system: clear the site, create a draft plan of the area, and then create a final plan that included a drawing of the uncovered building. Weber also wrote descriptive notes about the spaces and the objects found inside. Nonetheless, Weber's methods ultimately focused on treasure hunting.

Uncovered during Weber's tenure was the Praedia of Julia Felix, a complex that included a bath, a series of shops, and dining and reception rooms. By documenting the commercial complex in the same way monumental buildings, such as temples, were documented, Weber showed common business buildings and homes were as important as large public structures.

The discovery of the Praedia of Julia Felix in 1755 motivated the king to continue the dig at Pompeii. Workers did not have to tunnel to access the complex, although they found evidence of previous tunneling left by ancient people after the 79 eruption. Workers in the 1700s simply dug excavation trenches.

THE PRAEDIA OF JULIA FELIX

The Praedia of Julia Felix, or the House of Julia Felix, takes up almost an entire city block. It is one of the largest properties in Pompeii. The praedia is considered a commercial complex because of writing archaeologists found on the front of the property. The writing describes rental opportunities for the shops and homes in the complex:

To let, in the estate of Julia Felix, daughter of Spurius: elegant baths for respectable people, shops with upper rooms, and apartments. From the 13th August next to the 13th August of the sixth year, for five continuous years. The lease will expire at the end of the five years.[5]

Like many buildings owned by wealthy residents, the Praedia of Julia Felix featured a large open-air courtyard.

TOURISTS AND CRITICS

The king of Naples was proud of the Vesuvian excavations and invited people to see the treasures and the dig sites. The excavation sites in Campania became an important stop on the Grand Tour, a trip through Europe traditionally taken by young, wealthy men. Some even left with souvenir pieces of Pompeii.

With the praise of the Pompeii excavations also came criticism. Visitors criticized Alcubierre for the destruction caused by his methods. German historian and archaeologist Johann Joachim Winckelmann referred to Alcubierre in a 1762 letter: "This man, who has absolutely no experience working with antiques, is to blame for the many disasters and the loss of many beautiful things."[6]

POMPEII IS IDENTIFIED

In 1763, the buildings excavated at La Civita were definitively identified as belonging to Pompeii when workers uncovered the inscription *Rei publicae Pompeianorum*. The inscription means "the commonwealth of the Pompeians."[7] The following year, Weber died, and a new excavation director came to help Alcubierre, Spanish engineer Francesco La Vega. La Vega further improved the archaeological methods undertaken at the site. He believed in uncovering each building completely, documenting the building's interior, and making sure visitors could see the entire structure. La Vega also believed in conserving the site, which was especially important due to the large amount of tourist traffic. He made sure to repair and maintain buildings.

After La Vega came aboard, workers uncovered Pompeii's large theater, followed by the Temple of Isis. The temple discovery was unprecedented. As modern researchers Colin Amery and Brian Curran noted, "never before

had a complete Roman temple been found so intact with its furnishings, decorative schemes, and even the tortured corpses of its priests, too laden with booty to escape Vesuvius' wrath."[8] Shortly after making the sensational find, La Vega was promoted to director of excavations at Pompeii, although he still reported to Alcubierre. Expanded excavations began to reveal the city's pattern of streets. The fancy Villa of Diomedes was

THE TEMPLE OF ISIS

The Temple of Isis was built in the 100s BCE and was dedicated to an Egyptian goddess. The worship of Isis was popular in the Roman Empire because it offered the possibility of an afterlife, which worship of the traditional Roman gods did not.

The temple was rebuilt after the 62 earthquake, which suggests it was important or had wealthy parishioners. It stands on a platform with a short flight of stairs. A large entrance leads to the inner room that holds the altar and the statue of Isis. The roof and parts of the porch columns have not survived, but most of the rest of the building still stands. Excavators removed the paintings, which can be seen in the National Museum in Naples.

Pompeii's theater had been in use for hundreds of years before the city's demise.

51

THE HOUSE OF THE SURGEON

The House of the Surgeon was built in the 200s BCE, making it one of the oldest homes in Pompeii. It gets its name from the iron and bronze surgical instruments found inside, including scalpels, probes, catheters, and forceps. Excavators also found instruments known as bone levers, which scholars believe were used to put fractured bones back into place.

The surgical instruments found in the House of the Surgeon were typical of surgical instruments used for centuries. The technology behind some of the instruments remained largely the same as late as the 1900s. The tools are displayed at the National Museum in Naples.

uncovered, containing furniture, decorations, and the bodies of 18 women and children.[9]

After Alcubierre's death in 1780, La Vega took complete control of the site. He subsequently found buildings known as the House of the Surgeon and the House of Sallust, the Gladiators' Barracks, the Temple of Jupiter Meilichios, and the Triangular Forum.

Pompeii's main temple dedicated to Jupiter featured grand columns and was damaged during the 62 earthquake.

6

Preservation, Not Collection

Excavation slowed at the end of the 1700s because of the political upheaval in Europe following the French Revolution (1789–1799). However, after Napoléon I took over France and conquered Naples, the pace of work at Pompeii quickened.

Interest in excavating Pompeii increased in the early 1800s following a regime change in Europe.

Napoléon I first installed his brother Joseph as king of Naples. Then, after sending Joseph to Spain to be king there, Napoléon I named his sister Caroline and her husband, Joachim Murat, as Naples' rulers. King Joachim and Queen Caroline controlled Pompeii, and the excavations there became a state priority.

POMPEII UNDER NAPOLÉON I

King Joachim increased the workforce at Pompeii to 624 people by 1813.[1] During his reign, the government purchased all of the property within Pompeii's boundaries. This prevented individuals from doing private excavations and removing the items they found. During the same period, workers made their first major effort to excavate the city walls. Excavation also moved forward at the Forum and the amphitheater, and workers discovered the Basilica, the Temple of Apollo, and the Macellum.

Queen Caroline supported the Pompeii effort and frequently visited the site. She helped publicize the ancient city, writing to scholars and important European figures about the excavations. Caroline also supported the work of François Mazois, an artist who drew plans and sketches of the objects and buildings uncovered at Pompeii.

MORE DISCOVERIES

After Napoleón I's reign ended in 1814, the Bourbon dynasty—descendants of King Charles VII of Naples—returned to the throne. The Bourbon king, Ferdinand, did not care much about Pompeii. The work there slowed, the number of diggers dwindled, and land in Pompeii acquired by the government was put up for sale to raise money for further excavations. Ferdinand's successors showed varying degrees of enthusiasm for the excavations.

Nonetheless, workers uncovered many buildings during this second Bourbon period. The House of the Faun, found in 1831, caused the most sensation. It had a remarkable mosaic made of millions of stones that

THE AMPHITHEATER

Pompeii's amphitheater was built in 80 BCE, making it the earliest surviving permanent amphitheater in Italy, even older than Rome's famous Colosseum. An arena measuring 219 by 113 feet (66.8 by 34.5 m) with a capacity of up to 15,000 people, it is smaller than the Colosseum.[2] The amphitheater was used for sports, gladiator contests, and spectacles involving wild animals. Events were advertised with posters painted on walls, and they attracted audiences from the surrounding areas. Spectators were sometimes unruly. A riot broke out in 59 that left multiple people dead, leading the government to prohibit games in Pompeii for ten years.[3] The measure was revoked following the 62 earthquake.

The Alexander mosaic covers approximately 150 square feet (14 sq m).

depicted the battle between Alexander the Great and Darius of Persia. Another significant find was the House of Marcus Lucretius Fronto.

People considered the house important because of its beautiful frescoes. The significance of the find is emphasized by the fact that the king himself came to Pompeii to watch the house's unveiling.

By this time, whole city blocks were being uncovered at Pompeii. Workers were digging systematically; they followed the streets rather than a haphazard path. Also, workers made the first attempts to restore building frameworks so wall art could remain where it was found. Still, some artworks, such as the piece at the House of the Faun depicting Alexander the Great, were removed and taken to the National Museum in Naples.

Photography was introduced at Pompeii in the middle of the 1800s. Previously, all images of the city, its excavation, and its structures were drawings and paintings. Some early photographs are the only evidence of artifacts that no longer exist. Also new was a railway line that brought tourists from Naples to Pompeii. For some important tourists, site officials would stage excavations, reburying valuable objects and then uncovering them for the celebrity guests.

CHANGE IN ITALY AND POMPEII

In 1860, Giuseppe Garibaldi removed the Bourbons from Naples as part of the Italian unification effort that resulted in the establishment of the Kingdom of Italy under Victor Emmanuel II. Garibaldi chose his friend Alexandre Dumas to run the excavations at Pompeii and to direct the National Museum in Naples. Dumas's main contribution was the cataloging of the museum's collection of erotic art, much of which consisted of objects and frescoes from Pompeii.

After Dumas resigned his post that same year, Victor Emmanuel II hired Italian archaeologist Giuseppe Fiorelli for the job. Fiorelli brought a new perspective to Pompeii, aiming to study and document finds in addition to making sure they were protected and maintained. More significantly, Fiorelli did not want objects and murals removed and taken to Naples. He wanted

Dumas is best known as the author of *The Three Musketeers*.

them left in their original locations so they could be studied within their historical context. For some of the moveable objects, Fiorelli created a small museum at Pompeii. His approach was far different from that of the original excavator, Alcubierre, who was interested only in bringing treasure to the king in Naples.

FIORELLI'S INNOVATIONS

In addition to keeping intact as much as possible at Pompeii, Fiorelli introduced other changes to the excavation methods used at the site.

GIUSEPPE FIORELLI

Giuseppe Fiorelli was born in 1823 in Naples, Italy. He was a professor of archaeology in Naples before he was placed in charge of Pompeii's excavations in 1863. Fiorelli is known for many of his methods, including pumping cavities in the volcanic debris with plaster to construct models of the human bodies that created the voids, studying archaeological sites layer by layer, creating an identification system for Pompeii's buildings, and trying to keep antiquities intact. Fiorelli published many works about his Pompeii findings and served as the director of the National Museum in Naples. He died in Naples in 1896.

Fiorelli's plaster cast technique gave archaeologists startling insight into the last moments of doomed Pompeians.

One change was to stop shoveling out buildings from the street level up. Instead, workers began digging from the top down, taking away one layer of earth at a time. Fiorelli wanted to get information about the collapsed upper stories and also learn about the different phases of the 79 eruption. He used this information to make restorations more accurate.

Fiorelli introduced a building identification system at Pompeii. He divided the city into nine regions, numbered each block of houses within each region, and then numbered each doorway. For example, V.10.1, the Roman numeral for five followed by the Arabic numerals for ten and one, indicated the fifth region, tenth block, and first doorway. This system is still used today.

Fiorelli is best known for the plaster casts he made of the victims of the 79 eruption. Fiorelli noticed hardened volcanic ash around the bodies of some victims. After the victims' bodies decomposed, empty, body-shaped spaces were left behind. Fiorelli poured liquid plaster into the cavities to create models of the victims. A man, woman, and two young girls were the first to be captured in this way. *Smithsonian Magazine* described Fiorelli's results:

> *By filling the holes with plaster, he created disturbingly lifelike casts of this long-departed Pompeiian family in its final horrifying moments. It was as though an eyewitness from antiquity had stepped forward with photographs of the disaster.*[4]

One of the best-known Pompeii casts is of a dog that twisted around as it tried to free itself from a chain during Vesuvius' blast. A cast of a little boy who was killed with his family when they hid from the volcano is so detailed it shows the child's eyelids. The casts provided archaeologists with information about how the people and animals died. They also provided information about the type of clothing worn by the people of Pompeii.

Though they only show the outlines of figures, many of the plaster casts of people and animals are incredibly detailed.

Conservation Takes Hold

Fiorelli's personal attention to the excavation of Pompeii came to an end in 1875. That year, he was promoted to the job of general director of Italian antiquities and fine arts and moved to Rome. At the time of his departure, approximately half of Pompeii had been excavated. Fiorelli estimated Pompeii would be completely uncovered within 60 years.[1] While his successors continued Fiorelli's systematic approach to excavation, they also dedicated themselves to preserving the site, making progress

By the late 1800s, many of Pompeii's large structures were uncovered, but there was still much work to do.

slower. The period following Fiorelli's departure became one of the busiest and most fruitful in the history of Pompeii's excavation

PRESERVATION CONTINUES

After Fiorelli left, the job of directing the Campanian excavations fell to his assistant, architect Michele Ruggiero. Ruggiero is known for beginning the restoration of more than 500 frescoes found on the walls of Pompeian houses.[2] Ruggiero tried to restore and preserve paintings, mosaics, and stuccos at the site. His method of conserving frescoes involved removing them and then reattaching them to either the reinforced ancient wall or a rebuilt wall.

Ruggiero left decorations inside the houses where they were. To ensure these items were preserved, his team began covering the buildings with roofs built of wood and tile. Prior to Ruggiero, most of the excavated buildings had no roofs. The original ones had collapsed under the weight of the ash and stones that had fallen upon them in 79. As a result, when a building was excavated, it remained open to the elements after having been buried and safe from the elements for centuries.

Pompeii's preserved artwork gives modern viewers an incredibly clear view of people from nearly 2,000 years ago.

However, not all excavated buildings received a new roof. Only buildings containing particularly good wall paintings were protected by a roof, and the roof tended to divert rainwater to unprotected structures, damaging and destroying other paintings. During Ruggiero's directorship, gardens in some of the houses were also restored.

Among the buildings restored during the Ruggiero era was the House of the Silver Wedding, named to honor the twenty-fifth wedding anniversary of the reigning Italian monarchs, which occurred the same year the building was uncovered. The House of the Silver Wedding received a new roof, and the atrium was rebuilt. The decorations

THE HOUSE OF THE SILVER WEDDING

The House of the Silver Wedding was not named for the objects found inside the building but rather for an event happening when it was discovered in 1893: the twenty-fifth, or silver, wedding anniversary of Umberto and Margherita, the reigning Italian monarchs.

The House of the Silver Wedding was built in the 100s BCE and is noted for its atrium, a central space with a rectangular roof opening. The house has tall ceilings and four tall, fluted columns support its atrium. It also has two gardens, one with an open-air pool and a bathhouse.

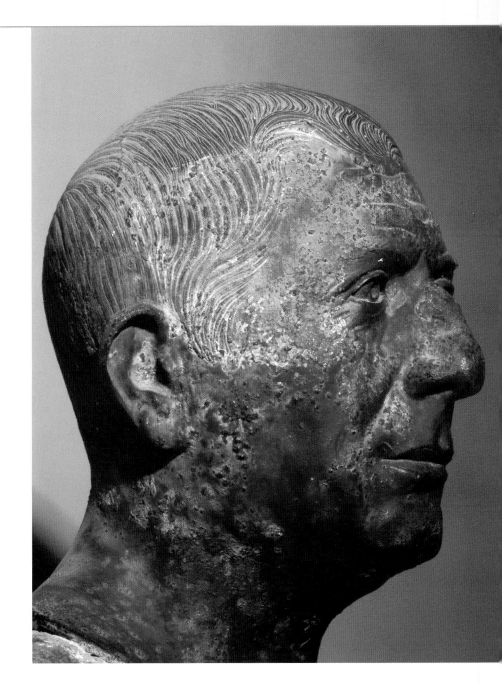

The home of
L. Caecilius
Jucundus
included a bust
of its owner.

and wall art remained in place rather than being taken to the National Museum in Naples.

In addition, Ruggiero discovered accounting documents in the house of banker L. Caecilius Jucundus. Giulio de Petra, who became director of the National Museum in Naples when Fiorelli went to Rome, deciphered the documents.

DIGGING
DEEPER

Roman Houses

The houses of wealthy citizens in Pompeii included an atrium, which is a courtyard open to the elements. The atrium let light and water into the house. In the atrium, there was a hole in the roof directly above a pool in the floor that would collect rainwater, which would drain into a cistern for storage. Once Pompeii was connected to a public water system by aqueduct, however, such pools became decorative only. Some became functional again after the 62 earthquake cut off aqueduct access.

Bedrooms, the living room, and the dining room all opened off the atrium. The houses also included an inner garden with a peristyle, a porch roof supported by columns. Homeowners grew vegetables in the peristyle garden. Sometimes, a bathhouse was found near the peristyle. Houses of the wealthy also had kitchens with counters, a hearth for cooking, and a sink with a drainpipe that fed into the drainpipe for the adjoining latrine, or toilet room. The wealthy frequently owned mosaics and installed them inside their homes. More modest homes had an entrance hall, a few multipurpose rooms, an open courtyard, and a vegetable garden. Some merchants lived in rooms behind their shops.

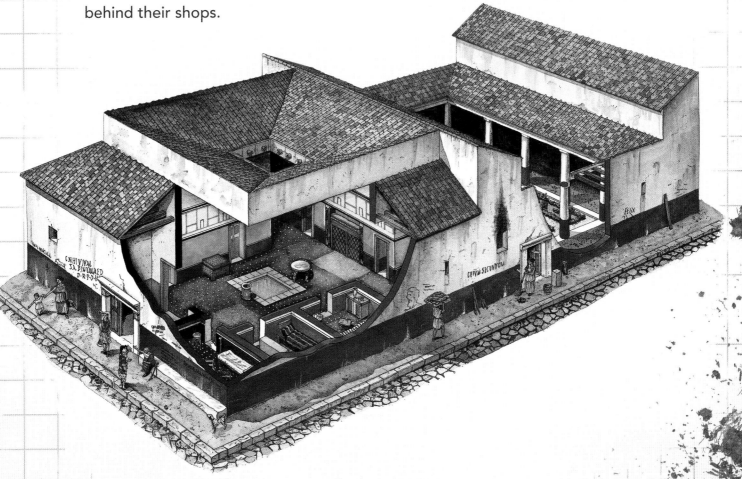

BEFORE 79

In the late 1800s, archaeologists began investigating the predisaster history of Pompeii. German archaeologists Frederick von Duhn and Louis Jacobi dug deeply into the earth in the Doric Temple and Forum areas. Another German archaeologist, August Mau, visited Pompeii in 1882 and spent years studying the city. He concerned himself with the history of the large and abundant paintings the ancient Romans put on their walls. The wall paintings were designed to make the rooms look bigger and brighter, masking the darkness within the house caused by the lack of windows other than open-air skylights.

The Romans made their frescoes directly on the walls of their rooms while the plaster was still wet. The style of the frescoes changed over the years. Mau identified four painting styles used by the ancient Romans over time, beginning in the 100s BCE and ending in the 100s CE. By characterizing the styles, Mau roughly dated the paintings. Mau's system is still used today in the study of these ancient Pompeian paintings.

De Petra took over the Pompeii excavations from Ruggiero in 1893. He was responsible for restoring roofs, covering atria and peristyles, and recreating inner gardens. During this era, the House of the Vettii and the House of the Golden Cupids were among those uncovered and restored. The reconstructions of those houses, along with the House of the Silver Wedding restored during Ruggiero's time, were the most successful undertaken during the latter part of the 1800s. All three of these houses are dramatic and extravagant. Because of the money and effort required, restorations happened to only the most remarkable buildings in Pompeii.

THE OUTSIDERS

During de Petra's administration, contractors began their first official digs at Pompeii. Gennara Matrone was one of the contractors. Matrone uncovered a suburb of Pompeii near the Mediterranean shore that contained shops. There were skeletons inside the shops, as well as gold jewelry, silver

THE FOUR STYLES OF ANCIENT ROMAN FRESCOES

In 1882, German archaeologist August Mau categorized Pompeii's wall paintings into four styles based partially on the writings of the Roman architect Vitruvius. The first style dates from approximately 150 BCE. It mainly involves recreating the look of a slab of marble or other natural stone. The second style, which dates from 90 BCE, features architectural details that appear three-dimensional. It shows windows and porticos that look out onto imaginary scenes. The third style, which began in approximately 25 BCE, features idealized landscapes with sacred objects in them. The landscapes are painted to look as though they are in a picture gallery. The fourth style, dating from 40 CE, combines the perspective of the second style with the scenic panels that make up the third style.

THE HOUSE OF THE VETTII

Known for its extravagant decorations, the House of the Vettii belonged to two wealthy citizens who were once slaves, Aulus Vettius Restitutus and Aulus Vettius Conviva. Scholars have theorized that once freed from slavery, the men made money as wine merchants, which allowed them to achieve aristocratic social status.

The house features art, including a painting of the god of fertility. The sitting room is known for its panels painted in a color known as Pompeii red and for artwork depicting cherubs. To this day, the house "gives the most complete impression of any structure in Pompeii," according to Bettina Bergmann, an expert on Greek and Roman art.[4]

vases, small bronze statues, and coins.

Unofficial digs took place, too. In 1895, Vincenzo De Prisco started digging. He was not part of the official excavation team, but he owned property in Campania. De Prisco excavated the ruins of a villa in Boscoreale near Pompeii and found a cache of 108 embossed silver vessels and 1,000 gold coins.[3] At that time, laws about private excavations were unclear, opening the door for ambitious private diggers. Before the authorities could intervene, De Prisco sold the silver items to Baron Edmond de Rothschild, who subsequently donated them to the Louvre Museum in Paris, France. A few years later, De Prisco dug into another villa and removed frescoes. De Petra asked the Italian government to form a commission to decide if it wanted to buy back the paintings taken from Boscoreale. The commission decided to purchase the paintings, but it was able to secure only a few for the National Museum in Naples. The Metropolitan Museum of Art in New York City purchased most of the paintings.

This loss of Italy's native antiquities, combined with accusations of financial mismanagement, led de Petra to resign from his posts as director of the National Museum in Naples and superintendent of excavations at Pompeii in 1900. He published a defense of his financial administration shortly thereafter. In 1906, de Petra returned to work at Pompeii for three additional years.

8

Discovery and Decay

Several new excavations were carried out during the 1900s. Italian historian Ettore Pais helmed the excavations for the first few years of the new century, taking over from de Petra. Under Pais's stewardship, the old handcart method of taking away debris as Pompeian buildings were excavated was replaced with a rail transport system, making the job more efficient.

The Triangular Forum became a focus of excavations in the early 1900s.

De Petra returned to the site in 1906, where he worked alongside a new superintendent of Pompeii, Antonio Sogliano. Sogliano wanted to learn about Pompeii's existence and development before it became a Roman city. He authorized the exploration of Pompeii underground. The in-depth studies took place in the Triangular Forum and the Civil Forum.

During Sogliano's administration, the preservation philosophy initiated by Fiorelli decades earlier continued. Uncovered frescoes and mosaics remained where they were found, requiring large amounts of time and money to protect them from the environment and from thieves. Sogliano also began the practice of placing lead strips into the plaster walls to keep water from seeping into the plaster.

UNCOVERING THE MAIN STREET

Excavation at Pompeii changed direction in 1910. Excavators had been working in the northern part of Pompeii. New superintendent Vittorio Spinazzola wanted to unite excavated areas in the southern quarters of the city with the center of the city.

Shops lined the Via dell'Abbondanza.

Bisecting the center of the city is a main road, which archaeologists named Via dell'Abbondanza, or "Street of Abundance," after they found a carving of the goddess of abundance on one of the street's fountains. Spinazzola wanted to uncover the road and fronts of the buildings along it. Archaeology scholar Jeremy Hartnett writes, "Spinazzola was driven by the belief that the paintings, graffiti, facades, and balconies that lined this street would provide a vivid image of life in this ancient town."[1] Spinazzola believed the excavation methods of the past ruined the second floors of buildings, along with the street-facing balconies protruding from them.

Large amounts of volcanic debris inside the structures were pressing on the building facades, challenging excavation efforts. Workers carefully

Counters with embedded jars for food are typical of Pompeii restaurants.

removed and replaced roofs and rebuilt all of the facades, including windows, shutters, doors, and other architectural features. The ceilings, floors, and frescoes inside the buildings were left where they were found and were repaired in place. Workers restored roofs and installed glass windows to protect the interiors. Spinazzola's excavation methods led to a deeper understanding of the building structures and also of their burial.

Spinazzola's methods also included using photography to document the work taking place in Pompeii. Still a fairly new technology, photography was used to an unprecedented extent during the Spinazzola administration.

Aside from Via dell'Abbondanza, other sites uncovered between 1910 and 1923 included Asellina's Thermopolium, a business akin to a take-out restaurant, and Stephanus's Laundry. The excavation uncovered commercial buildings in an archaeological site that had focused previously

ASELLINA'S THERMOPOLIUM

Also known as Asellina's Tavern, Asellina's Thermopolium was a place where patrons could buy ready-to-eat meals. The food was held in four large terracotta vessels integrated into a masonry counter at the front of the establishment. The building is located on Pompeii's main street, Via dell'Abbondanza. A staircase at the rear of the business led to guest rooms on the second floor.

The Villa of the Mysteries, which stands outside Pompeii's gates, is famous for having one of the best collections of frescoes in the Roman world. Particularly of note are the paintings in the *triclinium*, or dining room. The paintings have a deep red background and show a sequence of scenes thought to be initiation rites into the Dionysian Mysteries, a secret group honoring the Greek god of wine. However, some scholars contend the scenes depict an allegory about marriage. The paintings date to the first century BCE.

on residential structures. Still, a number of houses were also discovered.

THE LAST EXCAVATIONS

The last extensive period of excavation in Pompeii's archaeological history was from 1924 to 1961, a 37-year period in which archaeologist Amedeo Maiuri was the site's superintendent. The period was marked by many discoveries. Benito Mussolini, the dictator who rose to power in Italy in 1922, believed archaeology was a way to demonstrate Italy's past and future greatness. Funding increased dramatically.

Work continued on the excavations along Via dell'Abbondanza. Maiuri exposed the facades and also the spaces behind them. Work finished on the excavations of the amphitheater and the Large Gymnasium. Workers unearthed city walls and a nearby cemetery. They also discovered many other houses and sites. Uncovered just outside Pompeii was the Villa of the Mysteries, originally discovered in 1909 by a private excavator. The villa got its name from one of its frescoes, which some say depict secret rituals of a mysterious cult.

WORLD WAR II

After surviving the catastrophic eruption of 79 and making it through decades of excavation and preservation efforts, some of the buildings Maiuri and his predecessors unearthed were destroyed by bombing in 1943 during World War II (1939–1945). Allied forces believed German soldiers were in the area.

Reconstruction, excavation, and preservation are expensive, and not enough money was available from government funding or admission fees to complete the work. Maiuri sold volcanic material from the site to the company building a highway in the area. This led to buildings being excavated quickly and then

B-25 bomber aircraft stationed near Vesuvius gathered ash during World War II.

abandoned as workers moved to empty the valuable volcanic material from the next building. The funding problem, as well as inaccurate methodology and inadequate tools, resulted in the poor restoration of some houses.

In March 1944, Vesuvius erupted again, although it was not the same level of catastrophe as the eruptions of 79 and 1631. Still, 28 people died.[2] A nearby US airbase saw many of its aircraft destroyed by the hot ash. The eruption also slowed work at Pompeii.

THE POSTWAR PERIOD

After Maiuri's administration, much of the work at Pompeii focused on restoring and understanding buildings already uncovered, although some discovery and

THE 1944 ERUPTION

Early in 1944, small lava flows began appearing at the rim of Mount Vesuvius, and some of the lava spilled over the rim. The volcano quieted, only to erupt on March 13, 1944. Vivid orange lava spat from the volcano and flowed down the mountain in red rivulets. The eruption forced thousands of people who lived in the region out of their homes. The eruption also affected the combatants in World War II. The war was a clash between the Allies, including the United States, the United Kingdom, and the Soviet Union, and the Axis, including Germany and Italy. By 1944, US and British forces had invaded Italy and established an Allied airfield near Pompeii. Approximately 60 of their planes were damaged by the hot ash, cinder, and volcanic rocks Vesuvius rained on the region.[3]

excavation still happened. The digs that did occur were precisely targeted, unlike the wide excavations that were once standard. Digs focused on the stages of development of Pompeii in the centuries prior to its burial.

Pompeii faced the possibility of immediate demise when an earthquake struck Campania in 1980, killing more than 3,000 people.[4] In the aftermath of the quake, site superintendent Fausto Zevi took quick action to divert all funding from excavation to restoration. Many ruins were still closed to the public in 2013 as a result of the damage.

More chronicling of the area happened in the late 1990s. Workers used the latest digital technology to create computerized maps of the town and the region, as well as to catalog Pompeii's rapidly deteriorating treasures.

Also in the 1990s, Pompeii's funding woes eased somewhat when the Italian government passed a law that granted Pompeii autonomy from Italy's Ministry of Culture. Among other things, the 1997 law meant the archaeologists studying at Pompeii could keep all of the money they collected from admission fees instead of turning most of it over to the ministry. The law was deemed necessary to help provide the Pompeii superintendent with more money to preserve and restore decaying buildings.

DIGGING
DEEPER

Pompeian Skeletons

In the 1980s, the skeletal remains of 54 people who died in the 79 Vesuvius eruption were found in a basement storeroom under an agricultural depot in a suburb of Pompeii. According to Mary Beard, a professor of classics at the University of Cambridge, the skeletons have taught researchers a great deal about the Pompeian people and debunked some myths.

For example, one myth suggested ancient people were short. However, the people of Pompeii were taller than the average people of modern Naples. The skeletons found in the basement also dispel the myth that explorers brought back syphilis to Europe in the 1400s. Skeletons of twin children found in the basement show signs they were born with syphilis. The fact the twins survived until the eruption gives some indication about Roman society. The twins would have been quite unhealthy, so their family must have taken time and effort to care for them.

Some experts have taken issue with parts of Beard's analysis. She suggests the presence of middle-aged and elderly skeletons debunks the myth that ancient people did not live as long as modern people. However, the victims at Pompeii were elite members of society. They enjoyed better food and less harsh working conditions than most people of their day, likely living longer as a result. Improved nutrition may also account for their height. Beard's disagreement with other scientists about these facts highlights the importance of taking all of the available evidence into account when drawing conclusions.

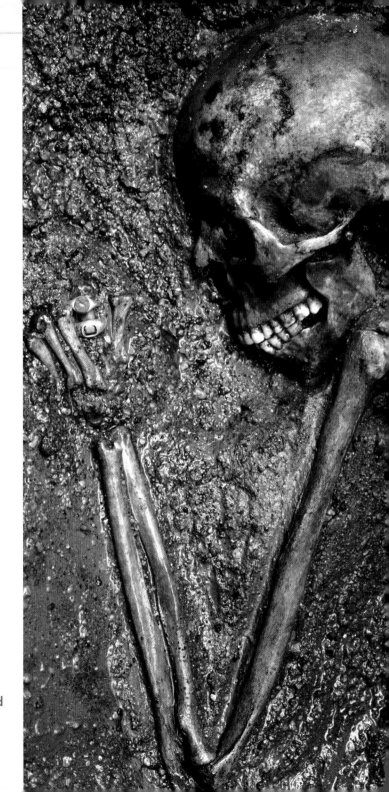

One skeleton at Herculaneum still had gold rings around one of its fingers.

9

The New Millennium

One November morning in 2010, workers noticed a pile of stone blocks lying in one of Pompeii's cobbled and rutted streets. The blocks had not been there the day before. The pile was all that was left of the Schola Armaturarum Juventus Pompeiani, which had collapsed during the night. This building is better known as the House of the Gladiators.

The collapse of the House of the Gladiators called attention to the issue of conservation at Pompeii.

The demise of the House of the Gladiators is an example of a bigger problem at Pompeii. A November 2010 newspaper article explained, "Experts believe that at present levels of maintenance the House of the Gladiators will certainly not be the last of Pompeii's treasures to tumble."[1] In fact, another collapse happened in 2012. The victim that time was a red-frescoed wall outside an unidentified ancient villa.

The collapses have focused worldwide attention on the Pompeii site, which is suffering from the consequences of its success. Since the mid-1700s, excavators and archaeologists have been successful in their quest to unearth much of the ancient city from the volcanic ash and rock that consumed it. Their finds have impressed the millions upon millions of people who have traveled to Campania to see and study them. However, the ruins were able to survive for nearly 2,000 years because they were protected underground. The exposure they

THE HOUSE OF THE GLADIATORS

A victim of collapse in 2010, the House of the Gladiators actually may not have housed gladiators. Scholars differ on the building's purpose. In a blog post the day after workers found the crumbled building, archaeologist Joanne Berry noted one scholar theorized the building was a school. She said another contended it was a place where gladiators kept their weapons. Archaeologist Frank Sear wrote that the building was a meeting hall for a military association.

have endured since being unearthed has taken its toll. In 1956, 64 individual sites were open to the public.[2] In 2013, only five were open at any one time because of damage.[3]

Reporter Esther Addley described conditions at Pompeii just after the collapse of the House of the Gladiators. She said:

> *In sections of the city enormous structural walls are propped up by wooden struts or steel supports while scaffolding and strips of orange plastic insist that visitors keep their distance. Roads closed to pedestrians have quickly been reclaimed by moss and grass, while small cracks in marble pedestals and brick walls have been colonised by weeds, and stray dogs growl at passing visitors. Protective Perspex screens covering priceless decorative or political wall paintings are missing in places. . . . In places large chunks of painted plaster are flaking away or already lie in crumbled pieces on the ground.[4]*

The problem of preserving the site is not new. Large-scale excavations ended in the 1960s because the site superintendent had his hands full caring for the buildings and objects that had been uncovered already. However, the problem has increased in significance while Italy's budgets for cultural sites have reduced. Authorities continue to grapple with how to solve the issue before the site disintegrates.

CONSERVATION INITIATIVES

The European Union (EU) has provided money to help conserve Pompeii. The organization provided 7.7 million Euros from 2000 to 2006 to be used on 22 restoration projects at the site.[5] Nonetheless, in 2008 the Italian government declared a state of emergency at Pompeii.

In 2012, the EU approved an additional 105 million Euros for restoration.[6] The EU grant is significant but still far less than the 260 million Euros former site superintendent Pietro Giovanni Guzzo estimated the site needs for a full restoration.[7] Work on the EU's Great Pompeii Project began in February 2013. The project aims to repair

Pompeii's overseers are trying to balance the economic and educational value of tourism with the fragile nature of the ruins.

and strengthen high-risk structures, build a drainage system to carry water away from the ancient buildings, and improve training of the site's staff.

Just after that work started, the United Nations Educational, Scientific and Cultural Organization (UNESCO), which monitors Pompeii and other heritage sites, issued a report on the ancient Roman cities. UNESCO's report indicated the Italian government was writing a new management plan for the ancient sites in Campania, progress had been made in regular site maintenance, and more professional staff had been hired to work on the EU project. Because of these steps, UNESCO did not recommend Pompeii's placement on its List of World Heritage in Danger. The list aims to make

ARCHAEOLOGICAL PRESERVATION IN ITALY

Italy has 47 World Heritage sites, more than any other country on the UN list.[8] Italy's World Heritage sites include the historic centers of Florence and Rome, the city of Verona, and the Amalfi Coast, in addition to Pompeii and its neighbors, Herculaneum and Torre Annunziata.

The country's historic sites require a great deal of conservation, but funding has been cut. In 2010, 2011, and 2012, a total of 1.42 billion Euros were cut from the budget of Italy's culture ministry.[9] At the same time, chunks of stone have fallen from the Roman Colosseum, part of the roof caved in at Nero's Golden Palace in Rome, and cracks have appeared in the ceiling of Florence's famed Duomo.

the international community aware of threats to world heritage sites and encourage corrective action.

New sources of investment have helped conserve similar ruins in Italy. At nearby Herculaneum, a 15-million-Euro investment by US computer billionaire David Packard boosted preservation efforts.[10] One controversial idea suggested limiting the number of visitors to Pompeii and renting the freed space as an event venue for large corporations.

WORK CONTINUES

As conservation and debate about Pompeii continues, so does the work of archaeologists and others who study the site. Jennifer and Arthur Stephens used modern technology to create a photo mosaic of the Via dell'Abbondanza that juxtaposes the current state of the street with pictures taken when it was excavated in the early 1900s. The Stephens' effort aims to produce a digital archive of the street.

The University of Bologna is using information from original surveys, as well as new surveys, to create virtual reconstructions and deepen understanding of Roman houses. Archaeologists from the University of Cincinnati took digital notes when reporting their digs, resulting in quicker information gathering as well as faster information distribution to other experts working on excavations. Digital notes are fast becoming a standard part of a modern archaeologist's tool kit.

NEW KNOWLEDGE UNCOVERED

Archaeologists continue to come away with new knowledge about Pompeii. Estelle Lazer, who used modern forensic techniques and statistical studies as she examined human skeleton remains from the site, debunked the myth that those who died at Vesuvius were young, old, sick, or female. She found the remains included both sexes of all ages and health statuses. The Archaeological Office of Naples and Pompeii discovered what was initially thought to be a throne in Herculaneum, but was later identified as an elaborate incense burner. Italy's National Institute of Optics disclosed in 2011 that some of the red color on many of Pompeii's walls—a color that led many elites of the 1700s to paint their dining rooms that characteristic shade—actually started as yellow and changed due to the chemicals and heat in the 79 eruption.

PRESERVING HERCULANEUM

Like Pompeii, Herculaneum was buried by Mount Vesuvius in 79. Unlike Pompeii, Herculaneum is in the midst of a conservation project that involves the local heritage authority, as well as the nonprofit Packard Humanities Institute and the British School at Rome. The Herculaneum Conservation Project has focused on improving roofs, drainage, and maintenance, in addition to making archaeological discoveries. Some see the public-private conservation project as a model Pompeii should follow.

Pompeii presents conservation challenges and also continued lessons to be uncovered about the ancient world. Classicist Mary Beard notes:

> It's terribly problematic, it's terribly hard to keep up. We'll never do as well with it as we want, but it is always helping us answer questions about the ancient world. It would be a sad day if all the questions were answered, wouldn't it?[11]

One-third of Pompeii remains underground, protected so future generations can find answers to their own questions about the ancient world.

Hundreds of years after their discovery, the ruins of Pompeii continue to provide archaeologists with new knowledge about the city and Roman society.

TIMELINE

80 BCE

Pompeii becomes a Roman colony.

79 CE

On August 24 and 25, Mount Vesuvius erupts, burying Pompeii, Herculaneum, and other nearby towns in Campania.

1592–1600

Domenico Fontana discovers Pompeii while digging a channel for a water diversion project.

1755

The Praedia of Julia Felix is uncovered during Karl Weber's tenure at the Pompeii site.

1763

Workers find an inscription proving the town they found under La Civita hill is Pompeii.

1831

The House of the Faun, complete with its elaborate mosaic depicting Alexander the Great, is discovered.

1863

Giuseppe Fiorelli becomes director of excavations at Pompeii. His plaster casts of Pompeii's victims become one of the most enduring artifacts from Pompeii.

1893

The House of the Silver Wedding is discovered.

1924

Amedeo Maiuri becomes the excavation director and seeks to leave all uncovered objects where they are found.

1943

Allied bombing damages Pompeii during World War II.

1980

An earthquake damages Pompeii, permanently closing many of its buildings.

2012

In March, the EU grants 105 million Euros for conservation efforts at Pompeii.

DIGGING UP THE FACTS

DATE OF DISCOVERY

Modern excavators first uncovered Pompeii between 1592 and 1600.

KEY PLAYERS

- Domenico Fontana first discovered Pompeii's ruins.

- Roque Joaquin de Alcubierre was a military engineer who began excavating Pompeii in 1748.

- Giuseppe Fiorelli, an archaeologist during the mid-1800s, was the first person to try to conserve archaeological finds in Pompeii.

KEY TECHNOLOGIES

Workers at Pompeii used shovels to dig, chisels and hammers to dislodge frescoes, and baskets to cart away earth. A rail system was put in place later to remove excavation debris. Documentation was originally done by hand. Artists supplied drawings. Photography was introduced in the mid-1800s. Now scientists use digital technology to record and distribute information, and computers are used to create three-dimensional reconstructions of buildings and objects.

IMPACT ON HISTORY

The burial of Pompeii suddenly erased a prosperous part of the otherwise peaceful Roman Empire from the map. Its excavation gave monarchs an opportunity to increase their prestige by looting artifacts, but eventually Pompeii became one of the first sites to be examined using modern archaeological techniques. Later eruptions by Vesuvius had further impacts throughout history, threatening whoever lived in the area at the time. This included the destruction of US military aircraft during World War II. Today, Pompeii is a focal point for those who wish to preserve the history of the ancient world.

IMPACT ON SCIENCE

Analysis of Pompeii's artifacts and architecture has taught scientists about ancient Roman houses, diets, health, religious rites, entertainment, fashion, household decoration, manufacturing, retail, slavery, gladiators, and daily life.

QUOTE

"It's a paradox of archaeology: you read the past best in its moments of trauma."
—*Andrew Wallace-Hadrill*

GLOSSARY

antiquity
An object, building, or work of art from the ancient past.

artifact
An object made by a human that has archaeological or historical interest.

atrium
An open-roofed entrance hall or central space in an ancient Roman house.

caldera
A bowl-shaped depression on a volcano caused by the collapse of rock after ejecting its supporting magma during an eruption.

excavate
To remove layers of earth from a site and document the artifacts found beneath the earth.

facade
The front of a building that looks out onto the street.

fresco
A painting drawn on the wet plaster of a wall or ceiling so the colors penetrate the plaster and become part of it as the wall dries.

inscription
Words written on or carved into an object.

lapilli
Rock fragments ejected from a volcano.

peristyle
A porch supported by a row of columns.

pyroclastic flow
A fast-moving current of hot gas and rock that comes from a volcano.

tephra
Ash particles that come out of a volcano in a pyroclastic flow.

villa
A large country house.

volcanology
The study of volcanoes.

ADDITIONAL RESOURCES

SELECTED BIBLIOGRAPHY

Amery, Colin, and Brian Curran Jr. *The Lost World of Pompeii*. London: Frances Lincoln, 2002. Print.

Berry, Joanne. *The Complete Pompeii*. New York: Thames & Hudson, 2007. Print.

Harris, Judith. *Pompeii Awakened: A Story of Rediscovery*. New York: I. B. Tauris, 2007. Print.

FURTHER READINGS

Compoint, Stephane. *Buried Treasures: Uncovering the Secrets of the Past*. New York: Abrams, 2011. Print.

Lindeen, Mary. *Ashes to Ashes: Uncovering Pompeii*. New York: Children's Press, 2008. Print.

Osborne, Mary Pope. *Pompeii: Lost & Found*. New York: Knopf, 2006. Print.

WEBSITES

To learn more about Digging Up the Past, visit **booklinks.abdopublishing.com.** These links are routinely monitored and updated to provide the most current information available.

FOR MORE INFORMATION

For more information on this subject, contact or visit the following organizations:

THE BRITISH MUSEUM

Great Russell Street

London WC1B 3DG

+44 20 7323 8299

http://www.britishmuseum.org

In 2013, the British Museum hosted an exhibition called *The Life and Death of Pompeii and Herculaneum*. The museum has antiquities from Pompeii.

SOPRINTENDENZA ARCHAEOLOGICA DI NAPOLI E POMPEI

via Villa dei Misteri

Pompeii, Italy

+39 081 85 75111

http://www.pompeiisites.org

This group is in charge of all archaeological work at Pompeii.

SOURCE NOTES

Chapter 1. Why Pompeii Matters Today

1. Doug Stewart. "Resurrecting Pompeii." *Smithsonian Magazine*. Smithsonian, Feb. 2006. Web. 18 June 2013.

2. "Pompeii." *CyArk*. CyArk, n.d. Web. 18 June 2013.

3. Salvator Ciro Nappo. "Pompeii: Its Discovery and Preservation." *BBC History*. BBC, 17 Feb. 2011. Web. 23 June 2013.

4. "Olympia: History." *Odysseys*. Greek Ministry of Education, Religious Affairs, Culture, and Sports, 2012. Web. 24 June 2013.

Chapter 2. The Burial of Pompeii

1. "Deadly Shadow of Vesuvius." *Nova*. PBS, 1998. Web. 1 June 2013.

2. "Visiting Pompeii." *Current Archeology*. Current Publishing, 28 Sept. 2007. Web. 1 June 2013.

3. Ibid.

4. Alison E. Cooley and M. G. L. Cooley. *Pompeii: A Sourcebook*. New York: Routledge, 2004. Print. 33.

5. Ibid.

6. "Visiting Pompeii." *Current Archeology*. Current Publishing, 28 Sept. 2007. Web. 1 June 2013.

7. "Vesuvius." *Volcano World*. Oregon State University, n.d. Web. 5 Feb. 2014.

8. John Noble Wilford. "Long Before Burying Pompeii, Vesuvius Vented Its Wrath." *New York Times*. New York Times, 7 Mar. 2006. Web. 1 June 2013.

9. "Visiting Pompeii." *Current Archeology*. Current Publishing, 28 Sept. 2007. Web. 1 June 2013.

10. Roger Ling. *Pompeii: History, Life & Afterlife*. Stroud, UK: Tempus, 2005. Print. 15.

11. Alison E. Cooley and M. G. L. Cooley. *Pompeii: A Sourcebook*. New York: Routledge, 2004. Print. 25.

12. Ibid. 37.

13. "Pompeii." *Encyclopaedia Britannica*. Encyclopaedia Britannica, 2013. Web. 1 June 2013.

Chapter 3. Digging Begins

1. Alison E. Cooley and M. G. L. Cooley. *Pompeii: A Sourcebook*. New York: Routledge, 2004. Print. 40.

2. "History and Eruptions: The Activity Between 79 AD and 1631." *Vesuvioinrete*. Vesuvioinrete, n.d. Web. 14 June 2013.

Chapter 4. Buried Cities

1. Ashleigh Murszewski. "Bones of the Victims at Roman Herculaneum." *Heritage Daily*. Heritage Daily, 30 Mar. 2013. Web. 17 June 2013.

2. "Herculaneum Theatre." *AD 79: Destruction and Rediscovery*. AD 79: Destruction and Rediscovery, n.d. Web. 17 June 2013.

Chapter 5. Pompeii's First Big Dig

1. "1748–1798." *History of the Excavation of Pompeii*. Soprintendenza Archaeologica di Napoli e Pompei, n.d. Web. 18 June 2013.

2. Lale Özgenel. "A Tale of Two Cities: In Search For Ancient Pompeii and Herculaneum." *Middle East Technical University Journal of the Faculty of Architecture* 25.1 (2008): 14. Print.

3. Ibid. 20.

4. Ibid. 21.

5. Alison E. Cooley and M. G. L. Cooley. *Pompeii: A Sourcebook*. New York: Routledge, 2004. Print. 171.

6. Colin Amery and Brian Curran Jr. *The Lost World of Pompeii*. London: Frances Lincoln, 2002. Print. 35.

7. Ibid. 36.

8. Ibid. 37.

9. Ibid.

Chapter 6. Preservation, Not Collection

1. Joanne Berry. *The Complete Pompeii.* New York: Thames and Hudson, 2007. Print. 50.
2. Ibid. 148.
3. "Amphitheatre." *AD 79: Destruction and Rediscovery.* AD 79: Destruction and Rediscovery, n.d. Web. 26 June 2013.
4. Doug Stewart. "Resurrecting Pompeii." *Smithsonian Magazine.* Smithsonian, Feb. 2006. Web. 20 June 2013.

Chapter 7. Conservation Takes Hold

1. August Mau. *Pompeii: Its Life and Art.* New York: MacMillan, 1899. Print. 29.
2. "The Discovery of Pompeii." *The History of Pompeii.* Pompeii.org.uk, n.d. Web. 21 June 2013.
3. Bettina Bergmann. "Seeing Women in the Villa of the Mysteries: A Modern Excavation of Dionysiac Murals." *Antiquity Recovered: The Legacy of Pompeii and Herculaneum.* Los Angeles, CA: J. Paul Getty Museum, 2007. Print. 237.
4. Ibid.

Chapter 8. Discovery and Decay

1. Jeremy Hartnett. "Abstract: Excavation Photographs and the Rediscovery of the Via dell'Abbondanza at Pompeii." *Archaeological Institute of America.* Archaeological Institute of America, n.d. Web. 24 June 2013.
2. Joanne Berry. *The Complete Pompeii.* New York: Thames and Hudson, 2007. Print. 29.
3. "Most Significant Eruptions at Mt. Vesuvius." *Quake Info.* University of California San Diego, n.d. Web. 24 June 2013.
4. "November 23, 1980: Southern Italy Rocked by Earthquake." *This Day in History.* History Channel, n.d. Web. 24 June 2013.

Chapter 9. The New Millennium

1. Esther Addley. "Neglected Ruins of Pompeii Declared a 'Disgrace to Italy.'" *Guardian*. Guardian, 11 Nov. 2010. Web. 25 June 2013.

2. "Saving Pompeii with the Help of Regional Funds: A Model for Italy and Campania." *European Commission*. European Union, 6 Feb. 2013. Web. 26 June 2013.

3. Ibid.

4. Esther Addley. "Neglected Ruins of Pompeii Declared a 'Disgrace to Italy.'" *Guardian*. Guardian, 11 Nov. 2010. Web. 25 June 2013.

5. "Saving Pompeii with the Help of Regional Funds: A Model for Italy and Campania." *European Commission*. European Union, 6 Feb. 2013. Web. 26 June 2013.

6. Ibid.

7. Susannah Palk. "Pompeii Faces Ruin for a Second Time." *CNN World*. CNN, 27 Dec. 2010. Web. 26 June 2013.

8. "UNESCO World Heritage Sites." *Italia*. Italian Government, n.d. Web. 26 June 2013.

9. Barbie Latza Nadeau. "Italy's Culture Falling to Ruins Amid Austerity Cuts." *Daily Beast*. Daily Beast, 19 Sept. 2012. Web. 6 Feb. 2014.

10. Peter Popham. "Ashes to Ashes: The Latter-Day Ruin of Pompeii." *Prospect Magazine*. Prospect Publishing, 28 Apr. 2010. Web. 26 June 2010.

11. Dan Vergano. "Digging Deeper: Archeologists Race to Show Pompeii Daily Life." *USA Today*. USA Today, 16 July 2009. Web. 26 June 2013.

INDEX

ABOUT THE AUTHOR

Diane Marczely Gimpel is a high school English teacher and freelance writer who formerly worked as a journalist at daily newspapers in southeastern Pennsylvania. Gimpel lives in the Philadelphia suburbs with her husband, Michael, and their two sons, Sean and Andy. This is her seventh book for young readers.